The 4 Step Success Mantra

Rashim Malhotra

Copyright © 2018 Rashim Malhotra

All rights reserved.

Contents

Introduction 3

Step 1 5
Be involved with your life 5

Step 2 11
Find Your Right Intention & Innovate 11

Step 3 18
Learn to compete in the correct way 18

Step 4 29
Go Out & Get Noticed 29

The 4 Step Success Mantra

Introduction

Success has no shortcuts, but there are ways to achieve it. Our life in itself is a long process. It follows a simple law of creation & growth. Anything that grows in this world has to go through its own process of growth. It can either be a living or a non-living thing. By non-living things I mean things which are not considered to be living but have a growth factor involved such as, Skills, Learning, Career, Relationships and many others. You think and name them yourself.

It is a universally accepted fact that any process which is NOT well understood and NOT well defined can never produce great results every time. In order to maximize success rate & minimize errors or failures, the basic requirement is to understand the whole process first and then define it properly.

When you look at an assembly line in a

manufacturing company, you can easily notice the same fact which I just mentioned above. These assembly lines have a very well defined processing path to ensure every part or component which is required to build the whole product is fitted at the right time and at the right place. In the end, the result comes as good quality products every time with no or close to zero defects.

Think what if the processing path of the same assembly line was not defined properly. The result would not come out with the same good quality and would also consist of a lot of errors, confusion and inefficiency of the work force.

I believe life Is not a race and also it is something more than just being a journey because in life almost everything has to go through some kind of a process to comply with the laws of creation & growth. We do not grow up in one day, growth in itself is a process.

As our life is concerned, I have always believed that life is a "Process". Anyone can achieve great results out of his efforts if he understands the whole process of life and defines all his action plans accordingly. This topic is quite big in itself that I already have published an entirely dedicated book over it "How To Become Your Own Best Version", which has a detailed description about how things happen in real life and how everything can be created at will just by understanding the true nature of life. But in this book we are only going to discuss and try to simplify the understanding about the "Process of Success" in as less as just four simple steps.

Step 1
Be involved with your life

"Involvement & Ignorance" are two sides of a same coin called "Life". The day we come into this world, we get involved with our life at the very first moment we come out of our mother's womb, alive. After that whatever we learn and do in our life is only subjected to our involvement with it. You learn to walk, talk and behave only according to your surroundings you are involved with every day and nothing at all that happen on the other side of the world out of the radius of your involvement. If you were born in a Hindu family then you are going to perceive your idea of life as the same family has about it and if you were born in a Catholic family, your idea of life will be according to their idea of life. You learn your first language that your family and people around you speak. You learn to walk on your feet because everyone around you walks the same way. Everything that you learn in the beginning stage of your life is completely a mirror image of your surroundings you are involved with. Imagine if you were to be grown up by wild animals like in the story of "Jungle Book", then what would you have learned, some kind of 'Wild Language' or the language you speak now?? I bet, if at that time we had seen our families and other people in our surroundings walking on their hands standing upside down and perceived it to be normal, then every one of us would have learned to walk standing upside down only and walking on your feet would have been considered as an extra talent.

This is a basic example about how our own involvement with everything is important to us. This does not stop here but goes on to the last moment of our life we spend here in this world. What we learn in school, college, workplace, sports fields and everywhere else, our own involvement is the only key which defines our level of mastery in our knowledge about everything in life.

Life is all about creation. We come in this world naked and empty handed. Everything we do in our life is created here only. Our involvement is the only key to what we create in our life, but we need to understand the other side of the coin as well. We also have an inverted side of involvement which is the key to non-creation and sometimes destruction as well, that is our "Ignorance". Everything in life from our academic performance, health or illnesses to our success or failure is a result of our own level of involvement and level of ignorance with the things that actually matter.

Ignorance, on the other hand is vast and endless like the space. While being involved with anything, notice, we ignore everything else happening in the world at the same point of time simply because we are unaware of it. It is only our involvement which truly makes us aware of everything we come across to.

There are two types of ignorance. One literally means the state of being unaware of things and information and the second type means 'deliberately' ignoring or disregarding important facts, things and information. If you look closely you will find hundreds of examples around which prove how ignorance may affect. A common example for the first type is you are sitting at home and are completely unaware of which train is about to reach the platform and which one has just left on the local train station. The second type refers to the example of a person who knows that the seat belt in his car is there for his own safety but still he ignores and rejects the idea of fastening the seat belt. Same goes for a person riding a motorcycle without putting on a helmet. These are one of the most commonly known mistakes in the world which people do even after being aware that these things can save their life. A lot of people make these type of mistakes every day. This is simply because of an ignorant behavior they forget to be involved with their own safety requirements.

In simple words, ignoring your involvement while doing anything leads to imperfection, misdirection or in some situations, disasters.

Our involvement is not just limited to our learning but it's importance extends to everything that really matters in our life. We humans are situational beings. We live our lives moving from situation to situation. Even in situations where no fear is involved, your involvement gives you a great opportunity to improve. In your personal and professional relationships, your personal involvement with people while communicating gives rise to more profound relationships filled with trust and respect rather communicating through email, phone or social media interactions.

Try and notice yourself that on occasions like anniversary or birthdays you must have been receiving good wishes from your well-wishers more through emails, texts or social media posts rather than people calling your number or coming in directly at your door. People around the world know it very well that social & personal relationships are an extremely important part of their life but still they tend to ignore their own personal interaction with people so easily as if it does not matter at all.

Everything gets better just by involving your personal self physically and mentally. While talking to your mother or father you become a son or a daughter, while talking to your kids you become a mother or a father, while talking to a friend you become a friend, while talking to your husband or wife you become his or her husband and wife, while talking to a client you become a professional. It's the same person, but acting completely different in different situations. Every situation gets better when you fully involve yourself as required in that moment. Now think for a few moments, what will happen if you begin to involve yourself while in every situation you face in your day to day life with a greater understanding of your responsibilities towards people and your own conscience? Don't you think this will provide you a lifetime opportunity to succeed in every single aspect of your life? Well, I certainly do think like that.

Before we go any further, I would like you take note of an important fact here that It will 'not' be a wise decision to determine involvement as good or ignorance as bad thing. Both have their own good and bad effects. Involvement can be productive when used with right things and it can also be destructive if used with wrong things, and same goes for Ignorance. It is good when used to ignore correct things which require to be ignored and it becomes worse when used to ignore wrong things which require to be considered carefully. If a right thing goes into the wrong hands, it becomes a wrong thing and if a wrong thing goes into the right hands, it becomes right. You can take an example of a gun. When it goes into the right hands it can provide security to people but when it goes into the wrong hands can take lives of many.

The main reason why we are talking about learning to be fully involved with life is because this is the only key which is going to be the initial building block of your success. It is your life and no one else's, so it is always going to be only you who will be responsible for all your success and failures. Every single thing that you achieve or fail to achieve is fully dependent on the level of your own involvement & level of ignorance.

Step 2
Find Your Right Intention & Innovate

Everyone has a desire to succeed but only a few make it to the top. There is a very simple reason behind it that, most of the people, now-a-days, have become ignorant and thus they ignore or forget to be involved completely in the process of finding the right intention behind their behavior towards their plan of action.

Your intention is an extremely important part in your way to success because it is only your intention which affects your behavior behind all of your plans of action. You may set your goals and you may try to focus on them too, but you are never going to achieve those goals until you control your behavior towards them. For example, you have set a goal to become an athlete but you do not control your behavior towards learning about & practicing your skill on a daily basis, instead remain lazy or tend to procrastinate because it includes a lot of hard work and stress. This way you are never going to be any closer to become an athlete or if you become one with lower levels of learning and practice, you are never going to become a great performing one.

The only flaw here is that you intended to become an athlete but you never intended to become the greatest performing athlete because if you had intended to become the greatest performing athlete then you would have automatically developed a feeling of obstinance and your behavior would have been driven by the same intention & obstinacy of becoming the best by learning and practicing your skills to the level of perfection, no matter how much hard work was required.

In order to find your right intention you must try to understand the answer to the "Why" about the end result of your goal. Innovation begins with understanding the needs and desires of the people in your surrounding because in the end it is going to be only people who will value you for what you are doing.

As an athlete, for example, try to understand 'Why' do you want to become the best or the greatest performer? Simply because when people see someone from their own society (where people share similar beliefs and values), is performing for their own state or country, they begin to expect a lot from his performance that the person would make them proud and if he does the same, they feel the pride. Finally this feeling of pride makes them love you back for what you do.

This principle is applicable in almost everything that you plan to do. You plan to set up a restaurant then people are going to judge you, not for who you are but only for what you are serving. If they like the quality and taste of the food being served in your restaurant, they will certainly love you back and make it a success or if they don't, they will turn their heads away.

Similarly If you do a job in any of the workplaces not necessarily a company but it can be a small shop, a garage or a restaurant, then also it becomes equally important for you to gain the trust and respect of your peers as it is important for any business owner or leader because if you need to succeed in your job then you have to have people who trust you and respect you for being good at your job. Your seniors would trust you only if you are so good at your work that they can rely upon you in different situations like in their absence or in times of deadline crisis. Your co-workers will trust you only when you become ready to help them at times when they are stuck with some things, professionally or personally. Your juniors and subordinates will trust you only when you help them learn and share your knowledge with them to help them develop without being 'a tough to handle' boss. Notice, firstly, all these situations require only you, acting differently in different situations and secondly, in all these situations you are dealing with only people at different levels.

I recently heard about a young boy through one of my close friends. Then I tried searching about him online and as I expected, I found a very good article describing his story on a website. I really felt that his success story is very inspiring and will also help many of you to understand what we are discussing here about innovation. I am sharing the same story with you.

"Living in Jaipur, India, Raghuvir belonged to a poor background. Owing to difficult financial circumstances, he had to give up his higher education after completing his school. To keep up with his financial needs, he began working for Amazon as a delivery boy, where he was getting only Rs 9,000 ($130 approx.) per month. Since he did not have a motor bike, he travelled by a bicycle to deliver at each customer's doorstep.

Travelling by a bicycle would quickly tire him out, so he often used to take tea breaks to unwind but finding a good tea vendor around would always be a challenge for him. He realized that there would be many other like him who would struggle to find a good cup of tea after a hectic day of work. This realization triggered the idea of his startup in is mind.

Raghuvir started working on the idea along with

his three other friends. He gradually built his network with the nearby vendors, soon interacting with over 100 vendors. The quality of the tea and delivery service he provided was so good that many vendors began to order tea from him. One of the biggest achievements came when became able to buy himself a motor bike.

Currently, Raghuvir has multiple tea delivery centers in Jaipur, and receives hundreds of orders every day on an average. His earning has even grown higher to Rs. One lakh every month, and is now a proud owner of four motorbikes being used for delivery purposes for the same service"

This story is not about how much money Raghuvir is making or how much he aims to make but this story is all about understanding even the smallest problems of people and coming up with a smart solution to it and establishing your idea successfully.

The bottom line from all these examples is you should always care about earning the love & trust of the people around you because if you notice then you can easily find out that almost all of your professional problems are directly or at some points indirectly related to people only and if you solve the people's problems then all of your professional problems will be automatically solved. For this you must try to understand the answer to any of the these questions which are:

1. How you can make them happy?
2. How you can add value in their lives?
3. How you can solve their problems?
4. How to give them a little more than the value of their hard earned money.

You must involve yourself in finding the answer to any of these questions. When you find an answer then it will enable you by suggesting a lot of new ideas to innovate something that can actually create a difference in people's life, and believe me, that will be the moment of the beginning of your own unstoppable journey for life because after this you will have a right & clear intention behind what you plan to do. In addition, this approach will make you stand apart from the crowd and will help you end all of your competition while making you a tough competition for others.

Step 3
Learn to compete in the correct way

Our world in present time is suffering from a widely spread "Genetic Disorder" called "Competition". The reason I believe that it is a 'Genetic Disorder' is that we have inherited this perception of competition in our behavior from many-many past generations and we have grown up in an environment where this perception was forced into our lives since the very beginning of our learning age. Everyone around us including our parents, teachers and mentors have always been teaching us to compete with each other by making us believe that this world is a place of competition and if we do not compete, we are sure of being left far behind everyone in life and thus, we can never succeed.

But I believe, life as we know it, shall not survive for a much longer time if people in the world keep competing with each other. We are 'social beings' (I never call humans "social animals") and our lives had evolved when we started coming together to form societies. A society literally means a group of people living together with similar values and beliefs. Thus, a society should be all about living together, with each other and for each other. Every person in the society must share 'universally' similar beliefs and values of relating to each other, trusting each other, respecting each other and helping each other, because this is the only way that we can make this world a better place to live for every single person in the society or for our future generations, and this can only be done when people in the society trust each other and love each other. Competition ruins everything slowly, because when people in the society start competing with each other they forget to love each other as they just want to prove themselves better than others around. When love stops shining in between two persons trust starts to fade away as they start to feel jealous, they start to feel insecure about their places in the same society, fear of being judged by people starts to take over their minds and a lot more things of similar nature begins to ruin and transform their whole belief system.

Just move your head and look around, you will find competition's existence in every possible place because almost everyone in today's world starts to teach their children to compete since the very beginning of their learning age and the same is further followed by schools, colleges, corporates etc. Arrogance, Rage, Hatred, Stress, Anxiety and almost every single negative emotion you ever come across to, can possibly be a direct result of only this perception of competing with each other. This way, competition can be highly destructive in nature.

But that does not mean that competition is completely destructive. This has a dual nature too. There is also a flip side of it which is highly progressive and constructive in nature. The flip side of competition comes into existence when you understand it more closely.

"Competition is not an act of winning over others but it is an act of striving to gain something."

Competition can be a very useful tool if used to support the process of your own skillful growth in life. It can increase your potential to an extent you could never even imagine sometimes. This also is a very helpful tool when you plan to increase the radius of your comfort zone. "Competition is not an act of winning over others but it is an act of striving to gain something". This statement reflects its purpose clearly if understood correctly. If you compete with people around you with a desire to win or to prove yourself better, then you can never be sure about winning every time. In fact, we all lose at many events in life. When you win, you feel good or great or perhaps on the top of the world, but when you lose you start to feel different negative emotions which I just mentioned above. Sometimes, these negative emotions can cause you a lot more stress than your mind & body can handle. You must have heard about many suicide cases of students due to failure in exams.

To use competition as a tool to support the process of your skillful growth you must learn to compete with your own self only and not others around you. You may learn as much as you want from others around you, not to compete with them but to increase your knowledge and understanding. Everyone has different levels in terms of knowledge, practice, proficiency, understanding and perceptions which can never even make you guess how much you exactly have to put in what you have, while trying to compete with the person next to you. You may do one or two things better than him but there is a great possibility that in many other things he will prove to be more efficient than you are. It all depends upon everyone's own level of involvement with the things they have learnt. But, when you start to compete with your own self continuously, then you give yourself an opportunity to grow your skills and abilities to an extent that no one would probably have imagined ever, simply when you do this then you stop caring about what others are doing and where do you stand. Your whole being becomes more focused on improving yourself day by day even if you have already crossed the best known levels of proficiency in the world in the same skill or field.

It all starts with a simple practice of creating a habit of asking yourself "Can I do better than this?" every time you achieve your desired result while practicing something. But, remember to ask yourself "Can I do better than this?" rather telling yourself that "I can do better than this." Simply because when you have questions in your mind, your mind gets curious about finding the answer which usually helps you more in finding the room for improvements and it has many subconscious triggers which it puts together with your quest for improvement without even letting you know. This self-competing approach can never possibly come to an end because there is always a room for improvement in everything in this world. Nothing is completely created or improved. This is the reason that you must never stop learning & practicing because if you keep on learning & practicing anything even if you become the best at it, it will give you more possibilities and reasons to improve as the radius of your imagination also grows with regular increase in your knowledge and understanding.

This understanding will further help you to clear the miss-understanding about

Finding a "Unique or Signature Strength".

Nowadays, people around the world are talking about "finding" your own "Unique or Signature Strength". Well, if you have found one then you may consider yourself as lucky, or else, if you have not found one then do not feel bad or confused about it because you stand with a huge number of people who could not find such strengths, even after trying hard they are just left with more confusion and nothing else.

Like everything in life, your unique or signature strength is also a matter of creation. You do not have to try to identify always what you are already good at because you always have the option to create it and become good at it. This can also be done anytime just by involving yourself with your own life a little bit more.

If you have noticed that since the beginning of this topic of self creation, we have been discussing the same thing. No matter if you are already doing something or you are about to choose what you are going to do, you just have to be involved in the process of improving your skill and keep your concentration on the same track of continuous improvement.

You need your unique or signature strength while dealing with the world around. Unique Strength, here, is a combination of two different words, Unique & Strength. The word 'Unique' refers to the 'skill' you create and develop within yourself and the word 'Strength' refers to the 'influence' of the same skill you impress on to the world around. Because any strength is only valued when it is applied and has an influence, otherwise any strength without its application does not matter at all.

Let me tell you a short story about a boy who created & grew his strength and without competing with anyone he became more successful than many in the same field.

"Ronak (name changed), an old friend of mine, was not much interested in studies so he quit after high school. Then after a couple of years of struggling to do something to support his life he finally adapted to an advice given by one of his friends to start up a ready-made garment store. So he opened a very small store of ready-made garments after arranging a little sum of money from his family and close friends. Though, in the beginning he would sell a few of his garments and earn some money, but he was not satisfied with the small earnings he made with it because after taking out some amount of money every month to payback the people he borrowed from he was left with a very small amount of money to save. He wanted to grow his small business in such a way that he could create a difference from the other stores but he did not know how to do it and what to do about it.

One fine day he saw a poster of a male fashion model. He was dressed up in a simple grey trouser and a white shirt with sunglasses but still looked very attractive. Suddenly something clicked in Ronak's mind and at the very same moment he decided what he is going to do to create a difference in his store. The next day he started watching fashion shows on the TV and internet to update his knowledge about latest trends in the fashion industry and also started noticing how all the models carried their outfits. He would also notice the film stars dressing styles while watching Hollywood as well as Bollywood movies. While updating his knowledge about the latest trends in the fashion industry he also started searching for garment whole sellers and manufacturers who could provide him the stock with similar trends as he wanted. After searching for a few days he found some places where he could get the stock of garments as he desired.

He then used each and every single penny he had saved and after stocking up his small store he started out with wearing some of the new trendy clothes himself and flaunting them in front of his friends and acquaintances. While doing this he always tried to dress up very carefully in the best possible similar way as he watched the fashion models and actors. He looked very attractive and as he expected, people started noticing him wherever he went. This slowly grew curiosity among people around him and whenever asked he would suggest them to come to his store if they wanted such attractive looking clothes.

His garments stock, in reality, was full of similar garments what every other store in the city was selling, but still he grew his customer count rapidly. The secret behind his popularity was not that he sold any special clothes to people but he served them with his "Self Gained Knowledge". When people used to visit his store, he simply greeted & treated every single person like his only best friend which made him quite a trustworthy fellow in people's mind. He used to suggest them clothes only with colors more suitable to their skin tones and design patterns keeping in mind about what kind of body shape they had without even letting them realize. He shared best of his knowledge about how to put on simple clothes and look more presentable and attractive like what type of shirts should be tucked-in and what types should be worn untucked. What kind of shoes they should wear while with different type of clothes. He, in reality, was just trying to make everyone who came to his store, happy and more confident about their own looks and personalities, which perhaps, almost no other store owner in the city was doing.

While searching for people and places from where he could get his stock, he was actually trying to locate the best quality of material similar to any costly branded products but at a reasonable price. He sold the best possible quality clothes at reasonable prices rather than trying to sell any special garments. All he did was, he made his service his 'Unique Strength', which he created by investing his time and involving himself in gaining the knowledge about how to look & feel confident. In return, people started loving buying garments from his store, and in any business if customers are happy with both your product quality and service quality then nothing can stop its success.

The same happened to him as well. In a few years this 23 year old guy when turned 30, his small store also turned into a big fashion outlet and later he also established his own garment manufacturing unit. His earnings grew along with the size of his small business.

Like in Ronak's story, every person in every field has the 'choice' of creating his own unique strength, and behind every unique strength there is always learning and practice. You just have to decide what you are going to do and then learning more and more about the same will surely open many ways to create your own 'unique or signature strength', because then "your skill becomes your uniqueness and your service becomes your strength".

So, stop fooling yourself in looking for your unique strength or what are you passionate about. Rather wasting your precious time to find out what are you good at, try to become good at something right now and create your own unique strength, which can add some kind of value in the lives of the people you are dealing with and earn the love & trust of the people than just money because people who will love your work, will surely be ready to give you any amount you ask for. Stop thinking about competing with anyone right now, and start thinking more about only to create yourself as best as you can in any discipline by competing with your own self every day to become better than what you were yesterday.

Step 4
Go Out & Get Noticed

You got involved with your way to success in the first step, you understood people's need and innovated something which can actually benefit them in the second step, you have now created your own unique strength with an undying attitude to keep improving by competing with your own self. What are you waiting for now?

Just go out and get noticed by presenting your products or skills to the people in the world. People are always waiting for those who can help them in solving their problems, who can give them moments of happiness and joy, or who can improve and add some kind of value in their lives.

Make a quick plan to & find the best way to reach out to the public. The world is full of possibilities and technologies today that has made it very easy for everyone to market their products or skills to the public. Find the right category of the people you have done all your work for. Your marketing strategy should begin with according to the nature of your products or services.

You can begin with listing on the e-commerce website most relevant to your products or services. You can run targeted advertisements on different social media platforms to create awareness among people about your work. There are a number of video publishing and sharing websites which work the best to educate people about how your products or service can create a difference in their lives by creating and uploading some nice video tutorials. If you have anyone who is an active blogger in your contacts then you can ask him to help you in marketing your products by including information about them in his blog or simply write and post an entire blog about it. You can do the same if you know how to write and post blogs on different blogging platforms. Try to find out the best suitable ways for yourself, I am sure when you will try, you will find many different ways to do so.

Remember that this is your life and this is your work and you are the only person on whom it depends for its success. Don't sit back and assume that people would automatically start noticing your work. It is never going to happen until you somehow attract a miracle. You have to take the responsibility to make it happen with all your possible efforts.

I would personally suggest that after doing all your hard work in finding the solutions to people's problems and creating stuff, If required, then give a manual demonstration or small presentation in your nearest local markets and public places, just do not feel shy and limit yourself because of your ego.

Always remember that everything gains its value only when it is being used or put to work. A high end mobile phone is completely useless until you use it or put it to work, no matter how great the hardware or software is there in it, no matter how many fabulous features are there in it. A currency note, no matter how much monetary value it holds, is going to remain just a piece of paper until it is used. Even a jet powered airplane cannot fly off or do anything on its own.

Everything in the world, no matter if it is constructive or destructive in nature, is useless until it is used or put to work. Now think about it once, after doing all of your hard work as was required to be done while creating what you have created "Ask yourself, what will happen if you remain inactive or don't do anything about being noticed by people?

Do you want to remain as a 'Useless' thing just like any other thing in the world which is there but has never been put to work?

Or, you want your products and services to 'Gain Value' in this world by just taking possible actions?"

Remember, no matter if you have an IQ of a

genius or possess multiple high level degrees or certificates, you cannot achieve anything without setting up your plan of action and then acting upon it without wasting any more time. It is always going to be your actions which will help you to gain some kind of value in this world.

Success has no shortcuts but it has ways to achieve it. All the people who have achieved success in their lives always have a story of dedication & hard work with their story of success. People do not become successful just by chance or by luck but they become successful because of their 'will' to do anything to get to their goals, no matter what.

Anyone can become successful as it has no set standards for only a few people. It is for all, but the only thing that you have to acknowledge is that success is a process with no shortcuts and any process works most efficiently only when it is well understood & efficiently defined. What you have just read is just a plan, but it is only your own involvement with it that can make it happen. So buckle yourself up tight because,

...**Your Time Starts Now.**

ABOUT THE AUTHOR

Born in 1983 in Gurgaon India, Rashim Malhotra, Author of "How To Become Your Own Best Version", worked in various industries such as Printing & Publishing, Automobiles and Human Resource Consulting. In 2012 he became an independent behavioral researcher after losing his motivation & passion in his job. After 6 years of his research about how things happen in real life he began his journey to share all of his findings & understanding about life with people through his books. He strongly believes that motivation developed from inside is far better and long lasting than received from any outside sources. All of his work concentrates on the same fact as he dreams of creating a society of self-motivated people, with an attitude of an unstoppable and performance oriented persona in everyone.

www.ingramcontent.com/pod-product-compliance
Lightning Source LLC
Chambersburg PA
CBHW031558210526
45464CB00003B/1340